Table of Contents

Glossary

Classifying. Putting similar things into categories.

Compound Words. When two words are put together to make one. Example: sandbox.

Consonants. Letters that are not vowels (every letter except a, e, i, o, and u).

Homonyms. Two words that sound the same but have different meanings and are usually spelled differently. Example: write and right.

Inference. Using logic to figure out what is unspoken but evident.

Main Idea. Finding the most important points.

Opposites. Things that are different in every way.

Phonics. Using the sounds letters make to decode unknown words.

Rhymes. Words with the same ending sounds. Example: lake and cake.

Riddles. A puzzling question.

Syllable. Word divisions. Each syllable has one vowel sound.

Syllabication. Dividing words into parts, each with a vowel sound.

Synonyms. Words that mean the same.

Vowels. The letters a, e, i, o, u and sometimes y.

Name: _____

Phonics

Some words are especially tricky to read because they have one or more silent letters. Many words you already know are like this, for example, **wrong** and **night**.

Directions: Draw a circle around the silent letter or letters in each word. The first one is done for you.

(w)rong	answer	autumn	whole
knife	hour	wrap	comb
sigh	straight	often	known
calm	taught	scent	daughter
whistle	wrote	knew	crumb

Directions: Draw a line between the rhyming words. The first one is done for you.

knew	try
sees	bowl
taut	stone
wrote	true
comb	song
straight	seize
sigh	home
known	great
wrong	taught
whole	boat

Name: _____

Phonics

Sometimes letters make sounds you don't expect. Two consonants can work together to make the sound of one consonant. The **f** sound can be made by **ph**, as in the word **elephant**. The consonant team of **gh** is most often silent, as in the words **night** and **though.** But it also can make the **f** sound as in the word **laugh.**

Directions: Draw a circle around the letters that make the **f** sound.

ele(ph)ant   cough   laugh   telephone   phonics

dolphins   enough   tough   alphabet   rough

Directions: Write the correct word from the above list to complete each sentence.

1. The **dolphins** were playing in the sea.

2. Did you have _____ time to do your homework?

3. A cold can make you _____ and sneeze.

4. The _____ ate peanuts with his trunk.

5. The road to my school is _____ and bumpy.

6. You had a _____ call this morning.

7. The _____ meat was hard to chew.

8. Studying _____ will help you to read better.

9. The _____ has 26 letters in it.

10. We began to _____ when the clowns came in.

Name: _____

Phonics

There are several consonants and consonant teams that make the k sound. They are the letter **c** (when followed by a, o, or u as in **cow** or **cup**, or by a consonant, as in **club**), the letter **k** (as in **milk**), the team of **ch** (as in **Christmas**), and **ck** (as in **black**). Also, the letter team of **qu** makes the **kw** sound (as in **quick**).

Directions: Read the following words. Draw a circle around the letters that make the **k** or **kw** sound. The first one is done for you.

a(ch)e   school   quite   market   comb

escape   camera   deck   darkness   equal

      Christmas   necklace   doctor   stomach   crack

nickel   skin   queen   thick   squirrel

Directions: Use your own words to finish the following sentences using words with the **k** sound.

1. If I had a nickel, I would _____ .

2. My doctor is very _____ .

3. A grey squirrel _____ .

4. If I had a camera now, I would take a picture of _____ .

5. When my stomach aches, _____ .

5

Name: _____

Phonics

The **sh** sound is usually made by the letter team **sh**. Sometimes it is made by the letter team **su** (as in **sugar**), the letter team of **ci** (as in **musician**), the team of **si** (as in **possession**), or the team **ti** (as in **station**).

Directions: Read the following words. Draw a circle around the letters that make the **sh** sound.

(su)re   wash   nation

delicious   action   rush

shine   special   attention   vacation   permission

Directions: Word Search. Find each word from the list in the puzzle and draw a circle around it. Eight words go across. Three words go down. One is done for you.

i	n	s	u	r	e	r	u	s	r	t
t	w	d	e	l	i	c	i	o	u	s
v	a	c	a	t	i	o	n	i	s	h
c	s	p	e	c	i	a	l	a	h	i
a	h	t	i	o	n	t	i	c	i	n
a	c	t	i	o	n	s	h	t	i	e
s	u	r	t	n	a	t	i	o	n	s
t	p	e	r	m	i	s	s	i	o	n
s	a	t	t	e	n	t	i	o	n	h

Name: _____

Phonics

In some word "families," the vowels have a long sound when you would expect them to have a short sound. For example, the **i** has a short sound in ch**i**ll, but a long sound in ch**i**ld. The **o** has a short sound in c**o**st, but a long sound in m**o**st.

Directions: Read the following words. Write the words that have a long sound under the word **LONG**, and the words that have a short vowel sound under the word **SHORT**. (Remember, a long vowel says its name — like the **a** in ate.)

old	odd	gosh	gold	sold	soft	toast	frost	lost	most
doll	roll	bone	done	kin	mill	mild	wild	blink	blind

LONG

SHORT

bone

doll

Name: _____

Review

Directions: Use words from the word box to fill in each blank. Each word is used only once. There is an example for each one.

knob	black	rush	laugh	bold	people
needle	school	host	autumn	delicious	handle
dolphin	most	quick	action	night	elephant

1. Write three words from the words box with silent letters: _____

   comb _____

2. Write three words with the **f** sound: _____

   alphabet _____

3. Write three words with the **k** sound: _____

   camp _____

4. Write three words with the **sh** sound: _____

   nation _____

5. Write three words with the long **o** sound: _____

   gold _____

6. Write three words in which le has the sound of **ul**: _____

   purple _____

Name: _____

Following Directions

Directions: On the top line by each picture, write the word from the word box that describes the person in the picture. Then, write a clue from the picture that helped you to decide.

chef	astronaut	teacher

_____

_____

Answer: _____

_____

Clue: _____

_____

chef	astronaut	teacher

_____

_____

Answer: _____

_____

Clue: _____

_____

chef	astronaut	teacher

_____

_____

Answer: _____

_____

Clue: _____

_____

Name: _____

Following Directions

Directions: Find each word in the word box and draw a circle around it. The first one is done for you.

canoe	t	c	a	n	h	s	p
chains	c	a	n	o	e	t	i
spider	h	s	o	n	s	c	r
star	a	t	i	s	t	h	e
tear	i	c	s	h	a	i	s
noise	n	t	e	a	r	n	t
chin	s	p	i	d	e	r	g

Directions: Write the correct word from the word box to finish each sentence.

1. I have to sew up a _____ in my shirt.

2. It is fun to make a wish on a _____ .

3. There was a _____ 's web over the door.

4. Our porch swing is held up by _____ .

5. We paddled a _____ down the river.

6. A lawnmower makes a lot of _____ .

7. I fell down and cut my _____ .

Name: _____

Compound Words

A compound word is usually divided into syllables between the two small words that were put together to make one word.

Directions: Read the words. Then divide them into syllables. The first one is done for you.

1. playground   play ground

2. sailboat   _____

3. nightmare   _____

4. dishpan   _____

5. pigpen   _____

6. outdoors   _____

7. beehive   _____

8. airplane   _____

9. cardboard   _____

10. nickname   _____

11. hilltop   _____

12. broomstick   _____

13. sunburn   _____

14. oatmeal   _____

15. campfire   _____

16. somewhere   _____

17. starfish   _____

18. birthday   _____

19. sidewalk   _____

20. necklace   _____

Name: _____

Compound Words

Directions: Read the compound words in the word box. Then use them to answer the questions. The first one is done for you.

sailboat	blueberry	bookcase	tablecloth	beehive
dishpan	pigpen	classroom	playground	bedtime
broomstick	treetop	fireplace	newspaper	sunburn

Which compound word means . . .

1. a case for books?   bookcase

2. a berry that is blue? _____

3. a hive for bees? _____

4. a place for fires? _____

5. a pen for pigs? _____

6. a room for a class? _____

7. a pan for dishes? _____

8. a boat to sail? _____

9. a paper for news? _____

10. a burn from the sun? _____

11. the top of a tree? _____

12. a stick for a broom? _____

13. the time to go to bed? _____

14. a cloth for the table? _____

15. ground to play on? _____

Name: _____

Homonyms

Homonyms are words that sound just alike but mean very different things. The spellings are usually different, too. For example, write and right.

Directions: Look at the pictures. Draw a circle around the word that tells what it is. The first one is done for you.

(nose) knows   ate   eight   sew   so

flower   flour   sum   some   hare   hair

four   for   I   eye   toe   tow

deer   dear   bear   bare   cents   sense

13

Name: _____

Homonyms

Directions: Draw a circle around the correct word to complete each sentence.

1. I am going to **right, write** a letter to my grandmother.

2. Draw a circle around the **right, write** answer.

3. Wait an **our, hour** before going swimming.

4. This is **our, hour** favorite book.

5. He got a **beat, beet** from his garden.

6. Our football team **beat, beet** that team.

7. Go to the store and **by, buy** a loaf of bread.

8. We will drive **by, buy** your house.

9. Have you **herd, heard** the news?

10. The dog is guarding a **herd, heard** of sheep.

11. It will be trouble if the dog **seas, sees** the cat!

12. They sailed the seven **seas, sees**.

13. We **made, maid** our beds this morning.

14. The **made, maid** will help with the cleaning.

15. We have **to, too, two** cars in the garage.

16. I am going **to, too, two** the zoo today.

17. My little brother is going **to, too, two**.

Name: _____

Vocabulary

Directions: Unscramble each word using the numbers below the letters to tell you what order they belong in. Write the word before its definition.

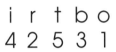

```
i  r  t  b  o
4  2  5  3  1
```

```
u  l  e  f
2  4  3  1
```

```
a  p  c  e  s        t  e  h  t  s  u  l
3  2  4  5  1        5  7  2  4  1  3  6
```

```
u  t  o  n  c  w  d  n  o
3  5  7  9  1  8  6  4  2
```

```
a  t  s  r  a  t  n  o  u
7  9  2  4  1  3  6  5  8
```

```
f  k  f  e  -  o  a  t
7  3  6  4     5  2  1
```

_____   A member of the team that flies a spaceship.

_____   A rocket-powered spaceship that travels between Earth and space.

_____   The material, such as gas, used for power.

_____   The seconds just before take-off.

_____   The path of a spaceship as it goes around Earth.

Review

Directions: Work the puzzle.

doctor

shark

by

dolphin

orbit

beehive

earthquake

whale

knows

hour

teacher

Across

3. The friendly gray animal with the pointed nose that lives in the ocean.
6. Compound word that means the trembling of the earth.
8. The path of a spaceship as it circles the Earth.
10. The unfriendly animal with many sharp teeth that lives in the ocean.

Down

1. The largest animal in the world. It lives in the ocean.
2. The homonym for nose.
3. A person who helps sick or hurt people.
4. The compound word that means a hive for bees.
5. A person who helps others learn.
7. The homonym for our.
9. The homonym for buy.

ANSWER KEY

This Answer Key has been designed so that it may be easily removed if you so desire.

GRADE 3 READING

Pull The Center Section From The Workbook

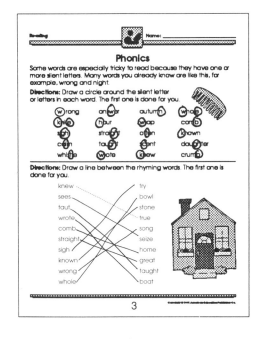

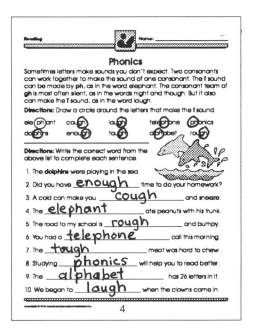

Phonics

There are several consonants and consonant teams that make the **k** sound. They are the letter c (when followed by a, o, or u, as in cow or cup, or by a consonant, as in club), the letter k (as in milk), the team of ch (as in Christmas), and ck (as in black). Also, the letter team of **qu** makes the **kw** sound (as in quick).

Directions: Read the following words. Draw a circle around the letters that make the **k** or **kw** sound. The first one is done for you.

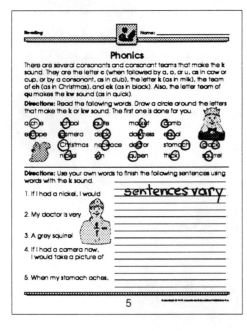

Directions: Use your own words to finish the following sentences using words with the **k** sound.

1. If I had a nickel, I would ___ *sentences vary*
2. My doctor is very ___
3. A grey squirrel ___
4. If I had a camera now, I would take a picture of ___
5. When my stomach aches, ___

5

Phonics

The **sh** sound is usually made by the letter team **sh**. Sometimes it is made by the letter team **su** (as in sugar), the consonant team of **ci** (as in musician), the team of **si** (as in possession), or the team **ti** (as in station).

Directions: Read the following words. Draw a circle around the letters that make the **sh** sound.

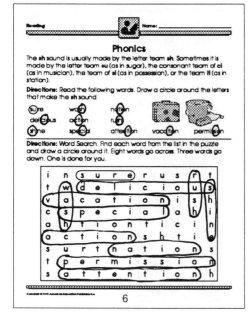

Directions: Word Search. Find each word from the list in the puzzle and draw a circle around it. Eight words go across. Three words go down. One is done for you.

6

Phonics

In some word "families," the vowels have a long sound when you would expect them to have a short sound. For example, the i has a short sound in chill, but a long sound in child. The o has a short sound in cost, but a long sound in most.

Directions: Read the following words. Write the words that have a long sound under the word **LONG**, and the words that have a short vowel sound under the word **SHORT**. (Remember, a long vowel says its name — like the **a** in ate.)

| old | odd | gosh | gold | sold | soft | toast | frost | lost | most |
| doll | roll | bone | done | kin | mill | mild | wild | blink | blind |

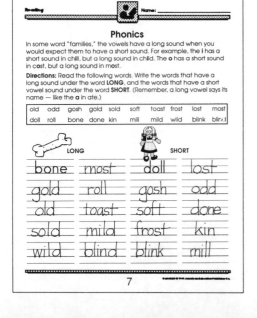

LONG		SHORT	
bone	most	doll	lost
gold	roll	gosh	odd
old	toast	soft	done
sold	mild	frost	kin
wild	blind	blink	mill

7

Review

Directions: Use words from the word box to fill in each blank. Each word is used only once. There is an example for each one.

knob	black	rush	laugh	bold	people
needle	school	host	autumn	delicious	handle
dolphin	most	quick	action	night	elephant

1. Write three words from the words box with silent letters:

comb ___ *knob autumn night*

2. Write three words with the **f** sound:

alphabet ___ *laugh dolphin elephant*

3. Write three words with the **k** sound:

camp ___ *black school quick*

4. Write three words with the **sh** sound:

nation ___ *rush delicious action*

5. Write three words with the long **o** sound:

gold ___ *bold most host*

6. Write three words in which **le** has the sound of **ul**:

purple ___ *people needle handle*

8

Following Directions

Directions: On the top line by each picture, write the word from the word box that describes the person in the picture. Then, write a clue from the picture that helped you to decide.

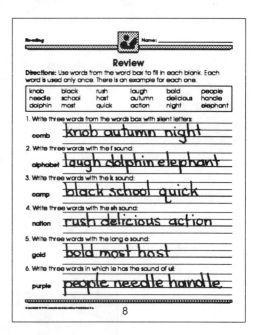

| chef | astronaut | teacher |

Answer: *astronaut*

Clue: *varies*

| chef | astronaut | teacher |

Answer: *teacher*

Clue: *varies*

| chef | astronaut | teacher |

Answer: *chef*

Clue: *varies*

9

Following Directions

Directions: Find each word in the word box and draw a circle around it. The first one is done for you.

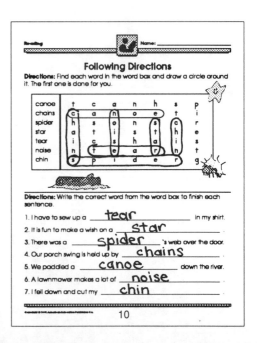

| canoe |
| chains |
| spider |
| star |
| tear |
| noise |
| chin |

Directions: Write the correct word from the word box to finish each sentence.

1. I have to sew up a ___ *tear* ___ in my shirt.
2. It is fun to make a wish on a ___ *star*
3. There was a ___ *spider* ___'s web over the door.
4. Our porch swing is held up by ___ *chains*
5. We paddled a ___ *canoe* ___ down the river.
6. A lawnmower makes a lot of ___ *noise*
7. I fell down and cut my ___ *chin*

10

Compound Words

A compound word is usually divided into syllables between the two small words that were put together to make one word.

Directions: Read the words. Then divide them into syllables. The first one is done for you.

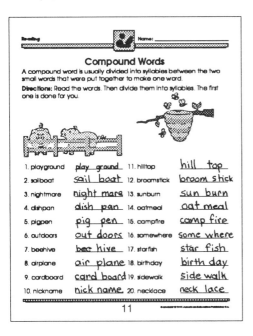

1. playground	play ground	11. hilltop	hill top
2. sailboat	sail boat	12. broomstick	broom stick
3. nightmare	night mare	13. sunburn	sun burn
4. dishpan	dish pan	14. oatmeal	oat meal
5. pigpen	pig pen	15. campfire	camp fire
6. outdoors	out doors	16. somewhere	some where
7. beehive	bee hive	17. starfish	star fish
8. airplane	air plane	18. birthday	birth day
9. cardboard	card board	19. sidewalk	side walk
10. nickname	nick name	20. necklace	neck lace

11

Compound Words

Directions: Read the compound words in the word box. Then use them to answer the questions. The first one is done for you.

sailboat	blueberry	bookcase	tablecloth	beehive
dishpan	pigpen	classroom	playground	bedtime
broomstick	treetop	fireplace	newspaper	sunburn

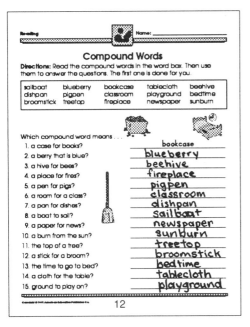

Which compound word means . . .

1. a case for books?	bookcase
2. a berry that is blue?	blueberry
3. a hive for bees?	beehive
4. a place for fires?	fireplace
5. a pen for pigs?	pigpen
6. a room for a class?	classroom
7. a pan for dishes?	dishpan
8. a boat to sail?	sailboat
9. a paper for news?	newspaper
10. a burn from the sun?	sunburn
11. the top of a tree?	treetop
12. a stick for a broom?	broomstick
13. the time to go to bed?	bedtime
14. a cloth for the table?	tablecloth
15. ground to play on?	playground

12

Homonyms

Homonyms are words that sound just alike but mean very different things. The spellings are usually different, too. For example, write and right.

Directions: Look at the pictures. Draw a circle around the word that tells what it is. The first one is done for you.

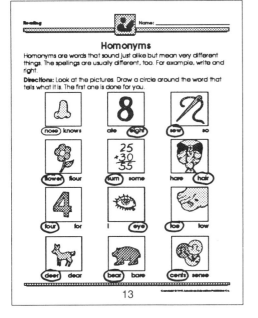

(nose) knows   ate (eight)   (sew) so

(flower) flour   (sum) some   hare (hair)

(four) for   I (eye)   (toe) tow

(deer) dear   (bear) bare   (cents) sense

13

Homonyms

Directions: Draw a circle around the correct word to complete each sentence.

1. I am going to right (write) a letter to my grandmother.
2. Draw a circle around the (right) write answer.
3. Wait an (our) hour before going swimming.
4. This is (our) hour favorite book.
5. He got a beat (beet) from his garden.
6. Our football team (beat) beet that team.
7. Go to the store and (by) buy a loaf of bread.
8. We will drive (by) buy your house.
9. Have you herd (heard) the news?
10. The dog is guarding a (herd) heard of sheep.
11. It will be trouble if the dog (sees) seas the cat!
12. They sailed the seven (seas) sees.
13. We (made) maid our beds this morning.
14. The made (maid) will help with the cleaning.
15. We have to, too (two) cars in the garage.
16. I am going (to) too, two the zoo today.
17. My little brother is going to (too) two.

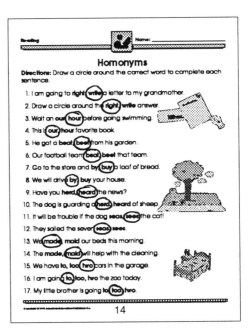

14

Vocabulary

Directions: Unscramble each word using the numbers below the letters to tell you what order they belong in. Write the word before its definition.

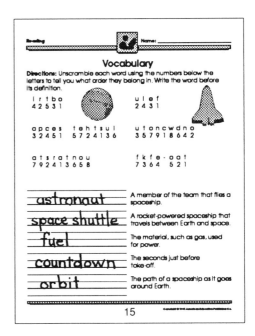

| l r t b o | u l e f |
| 4 2 5 3 1 | 2 4 3 1 |

| a p c e s | t e h t s u l | u t o n c w d n a |
| 3 2 4 5 1 | 5 7 2 4 1 3 6 | 3 5 7 9 1 8 6 4 2 |

| a t s r a t n o u | f k f e - o a t |
| 7 9 2 4 1 3 6 5 8 | 7 3 6 4   5 2 1 |

astronaut	A member of the team that flies a spaceship.
space shuttle	A rocket-powered spaceship that travels between Earth and space.
fuel	The material, such as gas, used for power.
countdown	The seconds just before take-off.
orbit	The path of a spaceship as it goes around Earth.

15

Review

Directions: Work the puzzle.

doctor
shark
by
dolphin
orbit
beehive
earthquake
whale
knows
hour
teacher

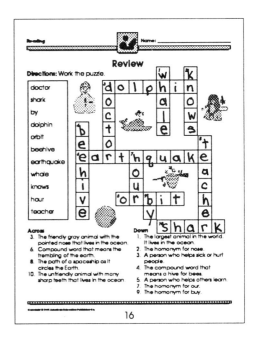

Across
3. The friendly gray animal with the pointed nose that lives in the ocean.
6. Compound word that means the trembling of the earth.
8. The path of a spaceship as it circles the Earth.
10. The unfriendly animal with many sharp teeth that lives in the ocean.

Down
1. The largest animal in the world. It lives in the ocean.
2. The homonym for nose.
3. A person who helps sick or hurt people.
4. The compound word that means a hive for bees.
5. A person who helps others learn.
7. The homonym for our.
9. The homonym for buy.

16

Sequencing

Directions: Look at the pictures. Read all of the sentences. Then write 1, 2, 3, or 4 by each sentence to tell the order of the story.

_3_ Dave washed the car with rags.

_2_ He put soap and water in a bucket.

_1_ Dave drove his car through a big mud puddle.

_4_ He rinsed the soap off of the car with a hose.

Sequencing

Directions: Read each story. Draw a circle around the phrase that tells what happened before.

1. Ben is very happy now that he has someone to play with. He hopes that his new little sister will grow up quickly!
   A few days ago . . .
   Ben was sick.
   (Ben's mother had a baby.)
   Ben got a new puppy.

2. Sarah tried to mend the tear. She used a needle and thread to sew up the hole.
   While playing, Sarah had . . .
   broken her bicycle.
   lost her watch.
   (torn her shirt.)

3. The movers took John's bike off of the truck and put it in the new garage. Next, they moved his bed into his new bedroom.
   John's family . . .
   (bought a new house.)
   went on vacation.
   bought a new truck.

4. Katie picked out a book about dinosaurs. Jim, who likes sports, chose two books about baseball.
   Katie and Jim . . .
   (went to the library.)
   went to the playground.
   went to the grocery.

Sequencing

Directions: In each blank, write the number 2, 3, 4, 5, or 6 to put the sentences in the correct order.

It is almost Valentine's Day . . .

_3_ Next, she cut the paper into heart shapes and decorated them.

_5_ She put names and addresses on the envelopes.

_1_ Sally wanted to make valentines for her friends.

_2_ First, she got out paper, glue, and scissors.

_6_ Finally, she put the valentines in the mailbox.

_4_ Then, she bought envelopes to put them in.

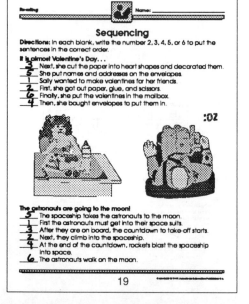

The astronauts are going to the moon!

_5_ The spaceship takes the astronauts to the moon.

_1_ First the astronauts must get into their space suits.

_3_ After they are on board, the countdown to take-off starts.

_2_ Next, they climb into the spaceship.

_4_ At the end of the countdown, rockets blast the spaceship into space.

_6_ The astronauts walk on the moon.

Sequencing

Directions: In each blank, write the number 2, 3, 4 or 5 to put the sentences in the correct order.

Building a Treehouse

_4_ At last they had a beautiful treehouse!

_2_ First they had to get wood and nails.

_1_ Jay and Lisa planned to build a treehouse.

_5_ Now they like to eat lunch in their treehouse.

_3_ Lisa and Jay worked in the backyard for three days building the treehouse.

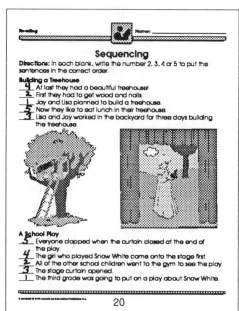

A School Play

_5_ Everyone clapped when the curtain closed at the end of the play.

_4_ The girl who played Snow White came onto the stage first.

_2_ All of the other school children went to the gym to see the play.

_3_ The stage curtain opened.

_1_ The third grade was going to put on a play about Snow White.

Classifying

Directions: Write a word from the word box that describes the words in the sentence.

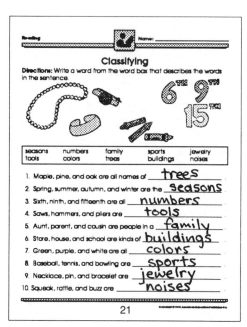

seasons	numbers	family	sports	jewelry
tools	colors	trees	buildings	noises

1. Maple, pine, and oak are all names of _trees_

2. Spring, summer, autumn, and winter are the _seasons_

3. Sixth, ninth, and fifteenth are all _numbers_

4. Saws, hammers, and pliers are _tools_

5. Aunt, parent, and cousin are people in a _family_

6. Store, house, and school are kinds of _buildings_

7. Green, purple, and white are all _colors_

8. Baseball, tennis, and bowling are all _sports_

9. Necklace, pin, and bracelet are _jewelry_

10. Squeak, rattle, and buzz are _noises_

Review

Directions: Read the story then follow the directions.

The Magnifying Glass

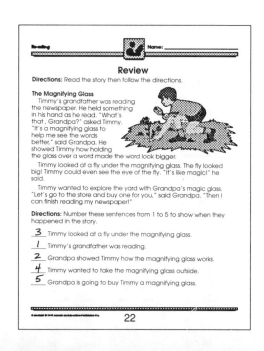

Timmy's grandfather was reading the newspaper. He held something in his hand as he read. "What's that, Grandpa?" asked Timmy. "It's a magnifying glass to help me see the words better," said Grandpa. He showed Timmy how holding the glass over a word made the word look bigger.

Timmy looked at a fly under the magnifying glass. The fly looked big! Timmy could even see the eye of the fly. "It's like magic!" he said.

Timmy wanted to explore the yard with Grandpa's magic glass. "Let's go to the store and buy one for you," said Grandpa. "Then I can finish reading my newspaper!"

Directions: Number these sentences from 1 to 5 to show when they happened in the story.

_3_ Timmy looked at a fly under the magnifying glass.

_1_ Timmy's grandfather was reading.

_2_ Grandpa showed Timmy how the magnifying glass works.

_4_ Timmy wanted to take the magnifying glass outside.

_5_ Grandpa is going to buy Timmy a magnifying glass.

Remembering What You Read

Directions: Read the story, then write words from the story to complete the sentences.

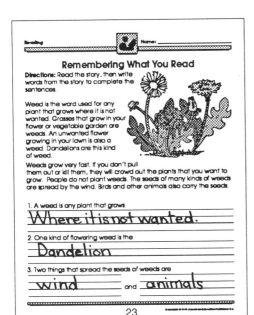

Weed is the word used for any plant that grows where it is not wanted. Grasses that grow in your flower or vegetable garden are weeds. An unwanted flower growing in your lawn is also a weed. Dandelions are this kind of weed.

Weeds grow very fast. If you don't pull them out or kill them, they will crowd out the plants that you want to grow. People do not plant weeds. The seeds of many kinds of weeds are spread by the wind. Birds and other animals also carry the seeds.

1. A weed is any plant that grows

<u>Where it is not wanted.</u>

2. One kind of flowering weed is the

<u>Dandelion</u>

3. Two things that spread the seeds of weeds are

<u>wind</u> and <u>animals</u>

23

Recognizing Details

Directions: Read the story, then answer the questions.

Giant pandas do not live in families like people do. The only pandas that live together are mothers and their babies. Newborn pandas are very tiny and helpless. They weight only five ounces when they are born — about the weight of a stick of butter! They are born with their eyes closed, and they have no teeth.

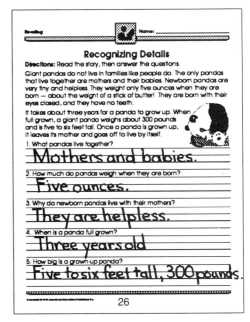

It takes about three years for a panda to grow up. When full grown, a giant panda weighs about 300 pounds and is five to six feet tall. Once a panda is grown up, it leaves its mother and goes off to live by itself.

1. What pandas live together?

<u>Mothers and babies.</u>

2. How much do pandas weigh when they are born?

<u>Five ounces.</u>

3. Why do newborn pandas live with their mothers?

<u>They are helpless.</u>

4. When is a panda full grown?

<u>Three years old</u>

5. How big is a grown-up panda?

<u>Five to six feet tall, 300 pounds.</u>

26

Remembering What You Read

Directions: Read the story, then answer the questions.

Each year, as the hours of daylight grow shorter and colder weather comes, many types of trees lose their leaves. The falling of the leaves is so regular and amazing that the entire autumn season has taken the name "fall."

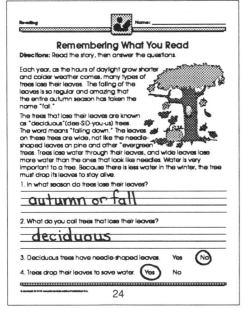

The trees that lose their leaves are known as "deciduous" (dee-SID-you-us) trees. The word means "falling down." The leaves on these trees are wide, not like the needle-shaped leaves on pine and other "evergreen" trees. Trees lose water through their leaves, and wide leaves lose more water than the ones that look like needles. Water is very important to a tree. Because there is less water in the winter, the tree must drop its leaves to stay alive.

1. In what season do trees lose their leaves?

<u>autumn or fall</u>

2. What do you call trees that lose their leaves?

<u>deciduous</u>

3. Deciduous trees have needle-shaped leaves.   Yes   (No)

4. Trees drop their leaves to save water.   (Yes)   No

24

Remembering What You Read

Directions: Read the story, then answer the questions.

The giant panda lives in the bamboo forests in the mountains of China. This is lucky, because bamboo is the panda's favorite food! Bamboo is a kind of woody grass. It grows to be very tall. Bamboo grows in tough shoots called stalks.

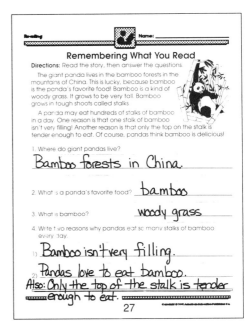

A panda may eat hundreds of stalks of bamboo in a day. One reason is that one stalk of bamboo isn't very filling! Another reason is that only the top on the stalk is tender enough to eat. Of course, pandas think bamboo is delicious!

1. Where do giant pandas live?

<u>Bamboo forests in China.</u>

2. What is a panda's favorite food? <u>bamboo</u>

3. What is bamboo?   <u>woody grass</u>

4. Write two reasons why pandas eat so many stalks of bamboo every day.

1) <u>Bamboo isn't very filling.</u>

2) <u>Pandas love to eat bamboo.</u>

Also: <u>Only the top of the stalk is tender enough to eat.</u>

27

Main Idea

Directions: Read about the giant panda. Then answer the questions.

Giant pandas are among the world's favorite animals. They look like big, cuddly stuffed toys. Sadly, there are not very many pandas in the world. You may have to travel a long way to see one.

There is only one place on Earth where pandas live in the wild. That is in the bamboo forests in the mountains of China. It is hard to see pandas in the forest because they are very shy. They hide among the many bamboo trees. It also is hard to see pandas because there are so few of them. Scientists think there may be less than 1,000 pandas living in the mountains.

1. The main idea is:

The giant panda is very shy.

(Giant pandas are rare, and live only in the bamboo forests in the mountains of China.)

2. What are two reasons that it is hard to see pandas in the wild.

1) <u>They are shy.</u> 2) <u>There aren't many.</u>

3. How many pandas are believed to be living in the mountains of China?

<u>1,000</u>

25

Main Idea

Directions: Read the story, then answer the questions.

Because bamboo is so important to pandas, they have special body features that help them to eat it. The panda's front foot is sort of like a hand. But instead of four fingers and a thumb, the panda has five fingers and an extra-long wrist bone. With his special front foot, the panda can easily pick up the stalks of bamboo. He also can hold them more tightly than he could with a hand like ours.

Bamboo stalks are very tough. To chew them, the panda has a big heavy head with large jaws and big back teeth. Here is how pandas eat bamboo: First, they peel the outside of the stalk. They do this by moving their front feet from side to side while holding the stalk in their teeth. Then they bite off a piece and chew it with their strong jaws.

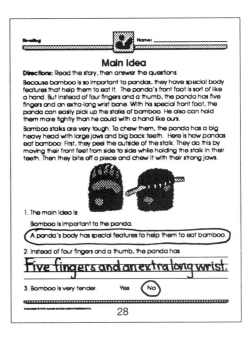

1. The main idea is:

Bamboo is important to the panda.

(A panda's body has special features to help them to eat bamboo.)

2. Instead of four fingers and a thumb, the panda has

<u>Five fingers and an extra long wrist.</u>

3. Bamboo is very tender.   Yes   (No)

28

Recognizing Details

Directions: Read the story, then answer the questions.

The giant panda is much smaller than a brown bear or a polar bear. In fact, a horse weighs about four times as much as a giant panda. So why is it called "giant"? It is giant next to another kind of panda called the red panda.

The red panda also lives in China. The red panda is about the size of a fox. It has a long, fluffy, striped tail, and beautiful reddish fur. It looks very much like a raccoon.

Many people think that giant pandas are bears. They look like bears. Even the word panda is Chinese for "white bear." But because of their relationship to the red panda, many scientists now believe that the panda is really more like a raccoon!

1. Why is the giant panda called "giant"?

Because it's much bigger than the red.

2. Where does the red panda live?   *China*

3. How big is the red panda?   *The size of a fox.*

4. What animal does the red panda look like?   *Raccoon*

5. What does the word panda mean?   *"White bear."*

Inference

Directions: Read the story, then answer the questions.

Many thousands of people go to the National Zoo each year to see Hsing-Hsing. Sometimes there will be as many as 1,000 visitors in one hour! Like all pandas, Hsing-Hsing spends most of his time sleeping. But because pandas are so rare, most people think it is exciting to see even a sleeping panda.

1. Popular means well-liked. Do you think giant pandas are popular?   *Yes.*

2. What clue do you have that pandas are popular?

Thousands of people go see them.

3. What do most visitors see Hsing-Hsing doing?   *Sleeping*

Remembering What You Read

Directions: Read the story, then answer the questions.

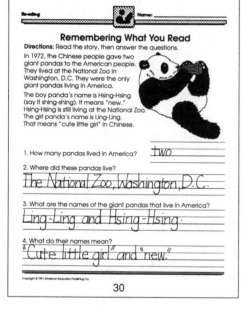

In 1972, the Chinese people gave two giant pandas to the American people. They lived at the National Zoo in Washington, D.C. They were the only giant pandas living in America.

The boy panda's name is Hsing-Hsing (say it shing-shing). It means "new." Hsing-Hsing is still living at the National Zoo. The girl panda's name is Ling-Ling. That means "cute little girl" in Chinese.

1. How many pandas lived in America?   *two*

2. Where did these pandas live?

The National Zoo, Washington, D.C.

3. What are the names of the giant pandas that live in America?

Ling-Ling and Hsing-Hsing.

4. What do their names mean?

"Cute little girl" and "new."

Review

Directions: Read the story, then answer the questions.

Ling-Ling and Hsing-Hsing lived next door to each other in a special Panda House in the National Zoo. They each had a large air-conditioned cage (the temperature is kept at 50 degrees Fahrenheit) and a sleeping den. Ling-Ling and Hsing-Hsing can played together in a big yard. The yard had bamboo trees growing in it.

It is very expensive to feed pandas. Besides bamboo, they also like rice, apples, bone meal, honey, carrots, cat food and dog biscuits, sweet potatoes, cantaloupes, and grass. It costs about as much to feed two pandas as it does to feed three elephants!

1. The main idea is:
   (Pandas have special needs.)
   Pandas eat a lot.

2. At what temerature do you need to keep panda cages?   *50 degrees.*

3. Name three things besides bamboo that pandas like to eat.

1) _____   2) _____

3) _____ *answers vary* _____

4. How expensive is it to feed two pandas?

As much as three elephants.

Notes

Notes

Sequencing

Directions: Look at the pictures. Read all of the sentences. Then write 1, 2, 3, or 4 by each sentence to tell the order of the story.

_____ Dave washed the car with rags.

_____ He put soap and water in a bucket.

_____ Dave drove his car through a big mud puddle.

_____ He rinsed the soap off of the car with a hose.

Name: _____

Sequencing

Directions: Read each story. Draw a circle around the phrase that tells what happened before.

1. Ben is very happy now that he has someone to play with. He hopes that his new little sister will grow up quickly!

    A few days ago . . .

    Ben was sick.
    Ben's mother had a baby.
    Ben got a new puppy.

2. Sarah tried to mend the tear. She used a needle and thread to sew up the hole.

    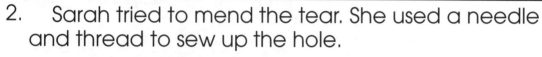

    While playing, Sarah had . . .

    broken her bicycle.
    lost her watch.
    torn her shirt.

3. The movers took John's bike off of the truck and put it in the new garage. Next, they moved his bed into his new bedroom.

    John's family . . .

    bought a new house.
    went on vacation.
    bought a new truck.

4. Katie picked out a book about dinosaurs. Jim, who likes sports, chose two books about baseball.

    Katie and Jim . . .

    went to the library.
    went to the playground.
    went to the grocery.

Name: _____

Sequencing

Directions: In each blank, write the number 2, 3, 4, 5, or 6 to put the sentences in the correct order.

It is almost Valentine's Day. . .

_____ Next, she cut the paper into heart shapes and decorated them.

_____ She put names and addresses on the envelopes.

__1__ Sally wanted to make valentines for her friends.

_____ First, she got out paper, glue, and scissors.

_____ Finally, she put the valentines in the mailbox.

_____ Then, she bought envelopes to put them in.

 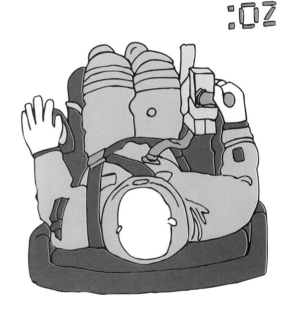

The astronauts are going to the moon!

_____ The spaceship takes the astronauts to the moon.

__1__ First the astronauts must get into their space suits.

_____ After they are on board, the countdown to take-off starts.

_____ Next, they climb into the spaceship.

_____ At the end of the countdown, rockets blast the spaceship into space.

_____ The astronauts walk on the moon.

Name: _____

Sequencing

Directions: In each blank, write the number 2, 3, 4 or 5 to put the sentences in the correct order.

Building a Treehouse

_____ At last they had a beautiful treehouse!

_____ First they had to get wood and nails.

__1__ Jay and Lisa planned to build a treehouse.

_____ Now they like to eat lunch in their treehouse.

_____ Lisa and Jay worked in the backyard for three days building the treehouse.

A School Play

_____ Everyone clapped when the curtain closed at the end of the play.

_____ The girl who played Snow White came onto the stage first.

_____ All of the other school children went to the gym to see the play.

_____ The stage curtain opened.

__1__ The third grade was going to put on a play about Snow White.

Name: _____

Classifying

Directions: Write a word from the word box that describes the words in the sentence.

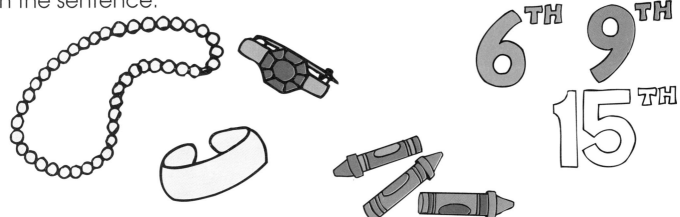

seasons	numbers	family	sports	jewelry
tools	colors	trees	buildings	noises

1. Maple, pine, and oak are all names of _____ .

2. Spring, summer, autumn, and winter are the _____ .

3. Sixth, ninth, and fifteenth are all _____ .

4. Saws, hammers, and pliers are _____ .

5. Aunt, parent, and cousin are people in a _____ .

6. Store, house, and school are kinds of _____ .

7. Green, purple, and white are all _____ .

8. Baseball, tennis, and bowling are _____ .

9. Necklace, pin, and bracelet are _____ .

10. Squeak, rattle, and buzz are _____ .

Name: _____

Review

Directions: Read the story then follow the directions.

The Magnifying Glass

Timmy's grandfather was reading the newspaper. He held something in his hand as he read. "What's that , Grandpa?" asked Timmy. "It's a magnifying glass to help me see the words better," said Grandpa. He showed Timmy how holding the glass over a word made the word look bigger.

Timmy looked at a fly under the magnifying glass. The fly looked big! Timmy could even see the eye of the fly. "It's like magic!" he said.

Timmy wanted to explore the yard with Grandpa's magic glass. "Let's go to the store and buy one for you," said Grandpa. "Then I can finish reading my newspaper!"

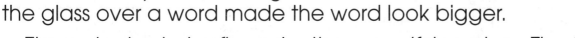

Directions: Number these sentences from 1 to 5 to show when they happened in the story.

_____ Timmy looked at a fly under the magnifying glass.

_____ Timmy's grandfather was reading.

_____ Grandpa showed Timmy how the magnifying glass works.

_____ Timmy wanted to take the magnifying glass outside.

_____ Grandpa is going to buy Timmy a magnifying glass.

Name: _____

Remembering What You Read

Directions: Read the story, then write words from the story to complete the sentences.

Weed is the word used for any plant that grows where it is not wanted. Grasses that grow in your flower or vegetable garden are weeds. An unwanted flower growing in your lawn is also a weed. Dandelions are this kind of weed.

Weeds grow very fast. If you don't pull them out or kill them, they will crowd out the plants that you want to grow. People do not plant weeds. The seeds of many kinds of weeds are spread by the wind. Birds and other animals also carry the seeds.

1. A weed is any plant that grows

_____

_____

2. One kind of flowering weed is the

_____

_____

3. Two things that spread the seeds of weeds are

_____ _____

_____ and _____

Name: _____

Remembering What You Read

Directions: Read the story, then answer the questions.

Each year, as the hours of daylight grow shorter and colder weather comes, many types of trees lose their leaves. The falling of the leaves is so regular and amazing that the entire autumn season has taken the name "fall."

The trees that lose their leave are known as "deciduous" (dee-SID-you-us) trees. The word means "falling down." The leaves on these trees are wide, not like the needle-shaped leaves on pine and other "evergreen" trees. Trees lose water through their leaves, and wide leaves lose more water than the ones that look like needles. Water is very important to a tree. Because there is less water in the winter, the tree must drop its leaves to stay alive.

1. In what season do trees lose their leaves?

_____

_____

_____

2. What do you call trees that lose their leaves?

_____

_____

_____

3. Deciduous trees have needle-shaped leaves.   Yes   No

4. Trees drop their leaves to save water.   Yes   No

Name: _____

Main Idea

Directions: Read about the giant panda. Then answer the questions.

Giant pandas are among the world's favorite animals. They look like big, cuddly stuffed toys. Sadly, there are not very many pandas in the world. You may have to travel a long way to see one.

There is only one place on Earth where pandas live in the wild. That is in the bamboo forests in the mountains of China. It is hard to see pandas in the forest because they are very shy. They hide among the many bamboo trees. It also is hard to see pandas because there are so few of them. Scientists think there may be less than 1,000 pandas living in the mountains.

1. The main idea is:

   The giant panda is very shy.

   Giant pandas are rare, and live only in the bamboo forests in the mountains of China.

2. What are two reasons that it is hard to see pandas in the wild.

   _____   _____

   1) _____ 2) _____

   _____   _____

3. How many pandas are believed to be living in the mountains of China?

   _____

   _____

   _____

Name: _____

Recognizing Details

Directions: Read the story, then answer the questions.

Giant pandas do not live in families like people do. The only pandas that live together are mothers and their babies. Newborn pandas are very tiny and helpless. They weigh only five ounces when they are born — about the weight of a stick of butter! They are born with their eyes closed, and they have no teeth.

It takes about three years for a panda to grow up. When full grown, a giant panda weighs about 300 pounds and is five to six feet tall. Once a panda is grown up, it leaves its mother and goes off to live by itself.

1. What pandas live together?

_____

_____

2. How much do pandas weigh when they are born?

_____

_____

3. Why do newborn pandas live with their mothers?

_____

_____

4. When is a panda full grown?

_____

_____

5. How big is a grown-up panda?

_____

_____

Name: _____

Remembering What You Read

Directions: Read the story, then answer the questions.

The giant panda lives in the bamboo forests in the mountains of China. This is lucky, because bamboo is the panda's favorite food! Bamboo is a kind of woody grass. It grows to be very tall. Bamboo grows in tough shoots called stalks.

A panda may eat hundreds of stalks of bamboo in a day. One reason is that one stalk of bamboo isn't very filling! Another reason is that only the top on the stalk is tender enough to eat. Of course, pandas think bamboo is delicious!

1. Where do giant pandas live?

_____

_____

_____

2. What is a panda's favorite food? _____

_____

_____

3. What is bamboo? _____

_____

4. Write two reasons why pandas eat so many stalks of bamboo every day.

_____

1) _____

_____

2) _____

_____

Name: _____

Main Idea

Directions: Read the story, then answer the questions.

Because bamboo is so important to pandas, they have special body features that help them to eat it. The panda's front foot is sort of like a hand. But instead of four fingers and a thumb, the panda has five fingers and an extra-long wrist bone. With his special front foot, the panda can easily pick up the stalks of bamboo. He also can hold them more tightly than he could with a hand like ours.

Bamboo stalks are very tough. To chew them, the panda has a big heavy head with large jaws and big back teeth. Here is how pandas eat bamboo: First, they peel the outside of the stalk. They do this by moving their front feet from side to side while holding the stalk in their teeth. Then they bite off a piece and chew it with their strong jaws.

1. The main idea is:

   Bamboo is important to the panda.

   A panda's body has special features to help them to eat bamboo.

2. Instead of four fingers and a thumb, the panda has

   _____

   _____

3. Bamboo is very tender.   Yes   No

Name: _____

Recognizing Details

Directions: Read the story, then answer the questions.

The giant panda is much smaller than a brown bear or a polar bear. In fact, a horse weighs about four times as much as a giant panda. So why is it called "giant"? It is giant next to another kind of panda called the red panda.

The red panda also lives in China. The red panda is about the size of a fox. It has a long, fluffy, striped tail, and beautiful reddish fur. It looks very much like a raccoon.

Many people think that giant pandas are bears. They look like bears. Even the word panda is Chinese for "white bear." But because of their relationship to the red panda, many scientists now believe that the panda is really more like a raccoon!

1. Why is the giant panda called "giant"?

_____

_____

_____

2. Where does the red panda live?

_____

3. How big is the red panda?

_____

4. What animal does the red panda look like?

_____

5. What does the word panda mean?

_____

Name: _____

Remembering What You Read

Directions: Read the story, then answer the questions.

In 1972, the Chinese people gave two giant pandas to the American people. They lived at the National Zoo in Washington, D.C. They were the only giant pandas living in America.

The girl panda's name is Ling-Ling. That means "cute little girl" in Chinese. The boy panda's name is Hsing-Hsing (say it shing-shing). It means "new."

1. How many pandas lived in America? _____

2. Where did these pandas live?
_____
_____
_____

3. What are the names of the giant pandas that came to America?
_____
_____
_____

4. What do their names mean?
_____
_____
_____

Name: _____

Inference

Directions: Read the story, then answer the questions.

Many thousands of people go to the National Zoo each year to see Ling-Ling and Hsing-Hsing. Sometimes there will be as many as 1,000 visitors in one hour! Like all pandas, Ling-Ling and Hsing-Hsing spend most of their time sleeping. But because pandas are so rare, most people think it is exciting to see even a sleeping panda.

1. Popular means well-liked. Do you think giant pandas are popular?

_____
_____

2. What clue do you have that pandas are popular?

_____
_____
_____

3. What do most visitors see Hsing-Hsing doing?

_____
_____

Name: _____

Review

Directions: Read the story, then answer the questions.

Ling-Ling and Hsing-Hsing live next door to each other in a special Panda House in the National Zoo. They each have a large air-conditioned cage (the temperature is kept at 50 degrees Fahrenheit) and a sleeping den. Ling-Ling and Hsing-Hsing can play together in a big yard. The yard has bamboo trees growing in it.

It is very expensive to feed pandas. Besides bamboo, they also like rice, apples, bone meal, honey, carrots, cat food and dog biscuits, sweet potatoes, cantaloupes, and grass. It costs about as much to feed two pandas as it does to feed three elephants!

1. The main idea is:

       Pandas have special needs.

       Pandas eat a lot.

2. At what temperature do you need to keep panda cages? _____

_____

_____

3. Name three things besides bamboo that pandas like to eat.

1) _____ 2) _____

_____

3) _____

_____

4. How expensive is it to feed two pandas? _____

_____

_____